THE ROOTS OF THE HATRED OF JEWS

ANTI-SEMITISM AS A UNIFYING ELEMENT OF ISLAM WITH THE RADICAL LEFT

Tel: +97254-8030648

Email Address: kobimnsil@gmail.com

Website: www.kobisha.com

ABOUT THE AUTHOR:

Kobi Shashoua is an author and a lecturer. Among his books you can find the most comprehensive book that exists to date bout the Israeli-Palestinian conflict "Israel: the truth, the whole truth and nothing but the truth." This book leads the reader chapter by chapter through the complex reality of the conflict and dissects the causes for the crisis, uncovers to the reader the true faces of the parties involved, and presents the tactics, the strategies and the true objectives, that lie below the surface. The author also wrote the book series: "Facts you should know about the Middle East".The book you are holding in your hands is from that series.

The author, who resides in Israel, which is located in the most dangerous neighborhood of the world, in the heart of the Middle East, shares with us the facts together with the insights and the unique understanding of the region where he lives. We invite you to take part in this journey from a safe distance.

FOREWORD:

For many, the Holocaust of the Jewish people through the systematic attempt to exterminate an entire nation is unfathomable. Wickedness in its full force has been active tirelessly to cleanse the human "stain" with the support and the encouragement of an entire population part of which participated, part of which chose to ignore and the majority that preferred to do nothing. But the Holocaust was, after all, a catharsis to persecutions, exterminations, plundering and deportations of the Jewish people countless times throughout history.

Many Jewish communities were destroyed during the centuries preceding the Holocaust. There were various strange pretexts but these didn't stop the riffraff from blaming Jewish communities. The Holocaust was in fact unavoidable and it was made possible due to the technological developments that enabled to optimize the genocide. The railroad tracks, the media, the development of modes of transportation, all these enabled to accelerate the rate of the extermination of the Jewish nation.

This fact was known and the Allies during World War II were aware of it but nevertheless it was at the bottom of their priorities.

At the end of World War II, when the dimensions of the disaster became clear, shame began to cover hatred in a thick shroud. It seemed that a new era of soul-searching and self-agony about the Holocaust committed against the Jews has started. In fact, shame covered the hatred but it bubbled and waited for the right moment to erupt in full force.

When the "Arab Spring" broke out in December 2010, huge waves of immigration started to flow from the Middle East toward the Western world. These waves carried the seeds of calamity that have just started to ripen against Western civilization and against the Jewish heretics – the enemies of Allah and of Islam. Thus the classic hatred of Jews in the Western countries combined with the idea of a religious war of the radical Islam. The amount of anti-Semitic events is at its peak. Jews are attacked everywhere from Australia, to Europe and to American countries. Jews are again defamed, accused of being the source of evil, of being the bearers of troubles. Anti-Semitism has reappeared and this time more forcefully.

The Jewish people have learned the lesson from the Holocaust and built a magnificent Jewish State out of the dessert. No wonder then that this country is constantly defamed, denounced, boycotted and condemned by the UN institutions that are controlled by dictatorships and by radical Muslim countries.

In this book we will be exposed to the immense measures of hatred that befell the Jewish people over the years of its existence and understand why anti-Semitism is not a passing phenomenon and is here to stay with us.

TABLE OF CONTENT

Hatred of Jews.

The blood libels.

The libel of "The Protocols of the Elders of Zion".

Blood libel in the Arab world.

The libel of the Palestinian organs.

Manifestations of hatred at present.

HATRED OF JEWS

Hatred of Jews is rooted among many nations around the world. Islam has joined this historical trend. For centuries in their past the church and Christianity have persecuted and tortured the Jews. There have been many accusations, starting with the handing over of Jesus to the Romans to various blood libels such as baking matzot[1] for Passover with the blood of Christian children, which is a particularly ingenious and successful blood libel, since it provides legitimization every year, toward Passover, to massacre with pleasure Jews wherever they are.

The persecutions and deportations from many countries continued for centuries. Nowadays, "The "Protocols of the Elders of Zion" are part of the curriculum in many Muslim countries. This is a blood libel that details the malicious Jewish plan to gain control over the world. These hateful anti-Semitic books are not sold on the black market or in obscure basements. You can purchase them only a few clicks away and join the cycle of hatred with scholarly excuses.

---

[1] matza is an unleavened flatbread that is part of Jewish cuisine and forms an integral element of the Passover festival, during which chametz (leaven and five grains that, per Jewish Law, can be leavened) is forbidden. (Wikipedia)

The Protocols of the Meetings of the Learned Elders of Zion by Elders of Zion and Victor E. Marsden (**Paperback** - Aug 3, 2009)

Buy new: **$18.99**

3 new from $14.98

Get it by **Thursday, Nov 12** if you order in the next 1 hour and choose one-day shipping.

Eligible for **FREE** Super Saver Shipping.

★★★☆☆ ☑ (64)

Self-source

"The Protocols of the Elders of Zion" are sold for an affordable price on the Amazon website. So what are you waiting for? Hurry up and order, and the next day they will be at your home (it is important to mention that on Amazon it was mentioned that this is a fabrication).

Hatred of Jews is a subject that is learned in many countries with governmental support. The peak record of hatred of the Jews happened when the Nazis came to power in Germany and during World War II. These events happened between 1933-1945 when the German regime, headed by the Nazi party, set for itself a target to deal once and for all with the Jewish "problem" in the easiest way – its abolishment. The abolishment almost succeeded and it ended with the extermination of 6,000,000 Jews and a total destruction of the Jewish community in Europe (90% of the Jewish community in Europe was annihilated). Much to the regret of many the work wasn't completed and there are some even today who dream about the day when they will be freed – of the Jewish problem.

By the way, did you ever think that using the word Nazi allows the Germans to evade their responsibility to some degree? After all, if a Nazi is not a German, and if there was no mobilization of the general German public, then perhaps only the Nazis fought in World War II against the Americans, the British, the Russians and the Allies, while the Germans did not take part in the war.

The previous volunteer whose aim was to destroy the "Zionist Entity" in the Middle East was none other than the former President of Iran, Mahmoud Ahmadinejad and his holy colleagues.

Many do not know what is it all about when the "Zionist Entity" is mentioned, but frankly, it sounds like something horrible, like some wicked entity, some hybrid creature, a frightening entity, a malicious conspiracy of the Jews……It does not sound at all like something that resembles a democratic country, and as such it is very easy to abolish it.

The conscious use of the term "Zionist entity" indicates something that should be cut off and the sooner the better. But this "Zionist entity" is in fact a democratic country called Israel that exists in miniature on an area that does not exceed 0.15% of the size of the Middle East.

Thus, beyond instilling hatred in the minds of the believers for hundreds and thousands of years, the Muslim as well joined the party, while all they wanted was to uproot the tumor called the "Zionist entity". The naive ones among us will say – what are you talking about? You are the aggressors, you are the ones who took control over the territories, and many believe it because this is what is   broadcasted, shown on the screen and published in the media.

But is that true? Of course not. We will discuss the issue of the "occupied territories" as well later on.

Burning Israeli flags has become a display in every event and demonstration, the shouting "slaughter the Jews" has become standard phrases in every self-respecting rally. Have you ever seen a demonstration of Jews where flags are burned? – And nevertheless, we are considered the aggressor, the barbaric side that slaughters children.

MAKES NO SENSE!

Books, movies and countless series have tried and are still trying to illustrate the horrors of the Holocaust and its extent. They will never succeed. There is no substitute for experience, and better this way. If you wish to read about the Holocaust, I am sure you will be able to find enough material in any way you choose. But if you wish to deny the Holocaust, you will find, unfortunately, enough attentive listeners. The decrease in the number of living witnesses makes the whole thing easier. Holocaust denial by anti-Semitics who hate Jews was joined, recently, by Muslims and Arabs, who consider it an important tool in delegitimizing the existence of the State of Israel.

According to their doctrine had there been no Holocaust it is likely that the State of Israel would not have been established.

Remember the saying by Edmund Burke:

"All that is needed for the evil forces to win is that good people will do nothing".

In order to understand the roots of the hatred of the Jews that eventually led to the Holocaust, it is necessary to dig into the depths of history. The truth? We will find the perpetrator quite easily: Judas Iscariot.

Judas Iscariot was one of the 12 apostles mentioned in the New Testament. According to Christian scriptures, he was accused of betraying Jesus and of handing him over to the Roman authorities. [1] Handing Jesus over led to his crucifixion and to his death in agony.

This betrayal was the basis for pogroms, persecutions, deportation, and for the maltreatment of the Jews for centuries. The story of the treason was the foundation for all the negative stereotypes that have been attached to the Jews.

---

[1] From Wikipedia under the entry: "Judas Iscariot".

And what if all that is not true?

On April 2006, the "National
Geographic" revealed the
"Gospel of Judas". [2] The
document, from the third or
the fourth century AD, is the
only remaining copy of the
Gospel. It is assumed that the
Gospel was probably written
in Greece by Gnostic
Christians [3] after the death
of Jesus. The Gospel contains
a different version that
relates to the life of Jesus. In
the Gospel it is told that Jesus
asked his faithful disciple, Judas Iscariot to turn him over
to the Romans and this is different from the concept that
prevailed that Judas betrayed Jesus by surrendering him
to the Romans out of his own initiative.

Gospel of Judas. Creator:
Worlfgang Rieger

This "new" information does not have the power to
challenge the belief entrenched in Christianity about the
story of Judas Iscariot`s betrayal of Jesus. [4]

(2) Gospel of Judas.

(3) A Christian denomination.

(4) An English translation of the Gospel is in the website:
http://www.nationalgeografic.com/lostgospel/_pdf/Gospelof_Judas.pdf

The book by Pope Benedict the 16th was published recently:

"Jesus of Nazareth Part II", in which he claims unequivocally that the Jewish people are not responsible for the death of Jesus of Nazareth! [5]

But let us not let the facts confuse us!

Early Christianity accepted the Bible but not the existence of the Jews. The Jews were the "chosen people" but they were replaced later on by a new chosen people "the Christians" because they failed to fulfill their mission. Jesus, the son of God, was chosen to lead the new people that replaced the Jews who sinned. As sinners they were condemned to live in degradation. I will introduce here a few examples of this concept among the Fathers of the early church:

In 387, the archbishop of Constantinople, John Chrysostom (347-407 AD), gave 8 sermons denouncing the Jews, here are some quotes: [6]

"The Jews sacrifice their sons and daughters to the devil", "They are worse than wild animals and for no reason they murder their offspring with their own hands in order to worship the devil, the enemy of our life", "They murdered the messiah and for that there is no absolution", "The Jewish synagogues are used as temples for idolatry and the seat of the devil", "God loathes them and in fact he always did. Ever since they murdered Jesus, God has not forgiven them for that".

Such wild incitement led, undoubtedly, to waves of violence, persecutions and pogroms that occurred in the course of history in the first and second millennium.

_____

(5) http://www.catholic.org/ae/books/review.php?id=40547

(6) Saint John Chrysostom (c. 347-407): Eight Homilies Against the Jews.

In some places this slander provoked people to violence, and in other places it led to other forms of persecution.

The hatred of Jews, encouraged by the Church, took shape over the course of history.

The pattern of behavior included publishing blood libels that attributed to the Jews ritualistic behaviors of the shadiest kind. Baking Matzot with the blood of Christian children who were kidnapped, killing children for ritualistic purposes etc.

The blood libels created a wave of pogroms and persecutions. The authorities cooperated and imposed on the Jews various decrees, which usually ended in deportation. This patter existed almost in every country where Jews lived, Jews who helped to develop the country and its economy. Deportation was the customary gratitude.

Following are a few examples of the deportation of Jews in the years 1000 till 2000 AD [7]:

- In 1290, the Jews were deported from England. About 16,000 left their possessions and their money behind
- In the years 1306, 1394, 1498, the Jews were deported from France. About 100,000 left their possessions and their money behind. (In 1306).
- In the years 1349 and 1360, Jews were deported from Hungary.

- In the years 1348 and 1498, Jews were deported from Germany.
- In 1381, Jews were deported from Strasburg. [8]
- In 1420, Jews were deported from Cologne. [9]
- In 1420, Jews were deported from Austria. 210 Jews were burned at the stake and the entire Jewish population was deported.
- In 1439, Jews were deported from Augsburg. [10]
- In 1445 and 1495, Jews were deported from Lithuania.
- In 1450, Jews were deported from Bavaria. [11]
- In 1453, Jews were deported from Breslau.
- In 1492, Jews were deported from Spain. About 200,000 were forbidden to take any valuables, jewelry, gold and silver.
- In 1492, Jews were deported from Sardinia.
- In 1493, Jews were deported from Sicily.
- In 1497, Jews were deported from Portugal.
- In 1541, Jews were deported from Napoli.
- In 1670, Jews were deported from Vienna.

In some of the cases the deportation was immediate, and stemmed from the desire of the authorities to loot the property and the belongings of the Jews. Many of them died and many never recovered.

Today, in the global era, when each one of us is in danger of being laid off, we react badly when we feel threatened. Imagine how you would react if it was   decided to deport you promptly and you would be left with no possessions and no money of your own, only with the cloths on your body.

MAKES NO SENSE!

---

(7) Source: Wikipedia, under the entry: "The deportation of Jews in Europe during the middle ages".

(8) Located in the Alsace region in the north east of France.

(9) The fourth largest city in Germany, known by its modern name Koln.

(10) Located in the Bavarian region and is one of the three oldest cities in Germany.

(11) A federal state in the southeast of Germany.

Apart from the deportations, there were also pogroms, decrees and persecutions.

Hereinafter is a short list of pogroms and persecutions: [12]

- The pogroms in the Rhineland, 1096.
- The Shepherds` pogrom in Spain and in France, 1320.
- The 1391 pogroms in Spain.
- The 1648 pogroms in Poland.
- The "Hep-Hep" riots in Germany, 1819.
- The "Storms in the Negev" in southern Russia, 1881-1882.
- The Kishinev pogroms, Russia, 1903.
- The "Recruits pogroms", Russia, 1904-1905.
- The "Black Hundreds" pogroms, Russia, 1905.
- The Petliura pogroms, Ukraine, 1919.
- The "Crystal Night", Germany, the night of 9-10th November 1938.
- The Farhud, Iraq, 1-2 June 1941.
- The Kielce pogrom, Poland, 4th July 1946.

This, of course, is only a partial list; the idea is not to create an endless shopping list, but to describe the extant of the hatred that eventually led to the Holocaust. This hatred not only did not fade over the years after the Holocaust, but it intensifies and is getting head strong again

Therefore do not be surprised that the United Nations convenes days and nights regarding the "aggression" of the State of Israel, while at the same time there are over 360 conflicts around the world in which masses are crushed, without anyone giving any attention to them or caring about them.

MAKES NO SENSE!

---

(12) Source: Wikipedia, under the entry: "Pogrom".

Do you detect here a recurring patter? Every so often, not long after the Jews accumulate money and possessions, they are persecuted, deported and killed. Lately it happened during World War II (1939-1945) and it seems that this patter attempts to repeat itself now that we have built a magnificent country out of the sands, the desert and the wasteland that were here. The American author, Mark Twain [13] described the region beautifully on his visit in 1867:[14] "...these deserts are empty, these faded mounds of wilderness...take that man-made hill covering the remains of an ancient settlement, Capernaum, take Tiberias, a foolish village that dozes off in the shade of its six lamenting palm trees; that desolate slope where the swine from the miracle tale galloped into the sea thinking, undoubtedly, that it had better swallow demons and ghosts and even drown in the water, than to go on living in such a place….take this monotonous, gloomy sailing-free lake, put it amidst a ring of yellow hills and low and steep banks….all these things – if these do not constitute excellent material for a lullaby that puts to sleep, then no lullaby is possible in the world."

If I were sarcastic, I would argue that the fulfillment of the dream of the Arabs in the region today is to throw us into the sea…without the possessions and the money.

In recent years the State of Israel is experiencing huge waves of immigration from many countries in the world. In the forefront of the waves of immigration are the Europeans headed by France. In coastal cities such as Ashdod and Netanya the French language is dominant. Many families are forced to leave their homeland and come to the State of Israel due to the increase in anti-Semitism combined with the waves of Muslim refugees that swarm to the European continent and who bear a blazing hatred of the Jewish people. Thus the European Jews find themselves outflanked by domestic haters of Jews on the one side, and the Muslims who hate the Jews on the other side. The lives of many Jews in

---

(13) An American author and humorist (1910-1935). Among his well-known books are: "The Adventures of Tom Sawyer", "The Adventures of Huckleberry Finn" (Wikipedia, under the entry: "Mark Twain").

(14) From Wikipedia, under the entry: "Pleasure Excursion to the Holy Land", translation from: "Mark Twain, a Pleasure Excursion to the Holy Land", Ariel publishing, Jerusalem 1999.

Europe has become abandoned. In recent years there were a few terrorist attacks against Jews in Europe, for instance the attack in the Hyper Cacher [15] on January 9th 2015. Moreover, the numbers of anti-Semitic incidents where Jews are beaten, persecuted and humiliated have increased.

The well-known expression "never again" [16] is trampled under the wheels of hatred and it is only a matter of time until the life of the Jews in Europe will remind of dark periods.

BLOOD LIBELS

The blood libels enabled to present the Jews as devil worshipers, as evil-seeking monsters, as scapegoats, and as an easy solution for the missing and the murdered. Just put the blame on the Jew and exempt yourselves from responsibility, and everybody will be happy to take revenge on the Jews and at the same opportunity to rob their possessions and their money.

The origin of the term "blood libel" is the most famous libel, in which it was claimed that the Jews use the blood of Christian children to bake matzos for Passover.

---

(15) From Wikipedia. The terrorist attack in the Jewish supermarket in Paris was a bargaining terrorist attack that happened on Friday, January 9th, 2015. A Muslim terrorist broke into the "Hyper Cacher", a branch of the Jewish owned supermarkets chain that sells kosher food products in the 12th districting in Paris, the capital of France. The terrorist took hostages from among the customers of the supermarket and the workers. After a few hours of blockade of the supermarket fighters from the counter terrorist unit broke into the supermarket and shot the terrorist to death. Four of the hostages were killed in the terrorist attack.

(16) "Never again" is an expression that describes the lesson the Jewish people have learned from the Holocaust according to which a crime like that – a cruel, systematic genocide – must not happen again.

(By the way, I personally love to eat not only matzos baked in blood but also many other foods. I usually order hamburger in blood sauce, I sprinkle blood on the pizzas instead of Tabasco sauce. In general, I usually flavor everything with blood). Although most of us are familiar with the Ten Commandments, the most severe prohibition is "Thou shalt not kill". I think that the Ten Commandments are not needed in order to understand that. The sanctity of life is the guiding principle for the Jews. This motif is deeply rooted in us and nevertheless, most of the blood libels revolve around Jews murdering the poor victim.

The first blood libels were invented in England and in France, and from there they spread to the rest of the European countries. [17]

The William of Norwich libel: this is the first blood libel that was spread in East England in 1149 by a monk called Thomas. The libel relates to an event that happened 5 years earlier.

The monk told that the body of a little boy named William was found in the forest with the symbols of "martyrdom" over it. The monk collected a number of evidences that "proved" that the Jews were involved in the matter: a maid in one of the Jewish homes told that she saw a boy bound. Another Christian told that he saw how the body of the boy was led to the forest. A converted Jew, who was a friend of the monk, told how each year the Jews gather and decide which town will sacrifice a Christian victim for Passover.

---

(17) The source of the descriptions of the blood libels in the following pages is Wikipedia, under the entry: "Blood libel".

The blood libel in Blois, France: the libel occurred in 1171. It began when a Jew dropped a package of processed leather when he met a Christian servant. The servant suspected that it was the body of a child and reported it to his master. The master who had disagreements with the Jews of the town, jump at the chance and updated the city`s authorities which cooperated with him. Although no corpse was found, the authorities

Simon torture: from the chronicle of Nuremberg (incunabula), 1493.

convicted all the Jews in the city. 31 of the city's Jews were locked up in a house and were burned alive.

The blood libel in Fulda, Germany: the libel occurred in 1235. The five children of a Christian miller were murdered at their home. The Jews were accused of the murder. 32 Jews were killed by the angry mob.

The blood libel in Lincoln, England: the libel occurred in 1255. The body of a poor child was found in a well. The well was considered to be a miracle worker and even to have the ability to cure blindness. The Jews were accused of the murder. One Jew was tortured and forced to confess. He was tied to the tail of a horse and later on he was raised to the gallows together with 17 other Jews.

The blood libel in Troas, Spain: the libel occurred in 1288. 13 Jews were sentenced to death by fire for the murder of a Christian child in order to use his blood for ritual purposes.

The libel of Simon from Trento, Italy: the libel occurred in 1475. A body of a child was found in a well at the house of a Jew. After the Jews were reported to the authorities, the family members were tortured and forced to admit that they killed the child. Some of the Jews who agreed to be baptized were decapitated, and the rest were burned alive while their flesh was torn off with burning hot tongs. 13 Jews were executed by torture and the rest of the Jewish community was expelled from the city.

The uprooting of the heart libel in La Guardia, Spain: the libel occurred in 1491, on the eve of the expulsion of the Jews from Spanish. In this libel, like in the blood libel in Blois, France, no body was found, although the Jews were accused of uprooting the heart of a Christian child for ritual purposes. The Jews were executed.

During the 18th and the 19th centuries many blood libels were spread in Poland and Russia, blood libels that led eventually to acts of murder and torture of Jews. Here are a few examples: during the blood libel in Poznan, Poland that occurred in 1736, four respectable Jews were tortured and murdered. During the blood libel in Zaslaw, Ukraine that occurred in 1747, 4 Jews were tortured to death. During the blood libel in Zhitomir, Ukraine that occurred in 1753, 12 Jews were scorched by fire, and while still alive they were dismembered.

The blood libels trials in Russia took place in the 19th century. In those trials Jews were accused of murder for ritual purposes. In all the cases, except for one, the defendants were acquitted of all charges. Nicholas the first, the future Czar, announced publicly in 1817 that among the Jews there were those who needed the blood of Christians. The only case in which Jews were convicted of murder for ritual purposes was in the town of Saratov, in 1852-1853. The 2 Jews that were convicted were imprisoned for 15 years.

The blood libels were refuted by a committee that was established for this purpose in 1855.

The Damascus libel, Syria: the libel occurred in 1840. The echoes of the libel aroused great interest in the world and caused the mobilization of the Jewish community around the world. Thomaso, a French monk, along with his Muslim servant disappeared after they posted a notice in the Jewish market in Damascus on February 5th 1840. The French consul in Damascus, Ulysse Ratti-Menton, who was anti-Semite, blamed the Jews for the disappearance.

A Jewish hairdresser was charged with the murder. The hairdresser was tortured and pleaded guilty while linking 7 of the community notables to the murder. Some of these Jews were tortured to death and others pleaded guilty. The Rabbi of Damascus, Rabbi Jacob Antebi, was tortured but did not succumb. A businessman named Haim Farhi, as well, was tortured and eventually released.

Bones were found In the Jewish Quarter, probably those of an animal. It was declared that those were the bones of the monk. The authorities started to search for the blood that was stored by the Jews. As a means of extortion they kidnapped and tortured 60 children aged 3-10 in order to extort admission of guilt from their parents.

The Rothschild family [18], with the assistance of the Austrian consul, managed to obtain documents that documented the case and published them in the world press. Public opinion raged. A delegation of French Jews arrived in Egypt to ask for the help of the Egyptian ruler Muhammad Ali. The 7 prisoners that survived were released after being tortured. The Governor of Damascus was executed.

In 1986 the Syrian Minister of Defense Mustafa Tlass published a book in which he reiterated the Damascus libel, according to which the Jews of Damascus murdered Thomaso the monk in order to use his blood. It looks like blood libels have not passed from the world (we will see later on examples from recent years).

The murder libel in the synagogue in Tisza Eszlar in Hungary: the libel occurred in 1882. A Christian girl named Esther Solymosi disappeared. The Jews were blamed for that. 15 Jews were prosecuted. 2 sons of the community Shamash were abducted and held by the church. The big brother was brainwashed. He testified in the trial that he saw through the keyhole how the Shohat of the community was slitting the throat of the young girl in the basement of the synagogue. The testimony was full of holes. The Hungarian author Karl Eotvas, from the defense, asked the judges to come to the synagogue in order to refute the testimony of the Shamash's son. The lock had no hole and it was impossible to see anything. The trial led to riots and pogroms in a number of towns and the government declared a military regime. Military units were sent to protect the Jewish communities.

At the end of the trial, all the Jewish defendants were acquitted and the appeals of the prosecution to the court in Budapest were rejected.

---

(18) The Rothschild family is a Jewish banking dynasty of German origin that has received over the years various noble ranks, both from the Austro-Hungarian authorities and from the British government. From Wikipedia under the entry: "Rothschild family".

The libel of the murder of the young girl in Polana Czech: the libel occurred in 1899. Anzaka Heroztova, a 19 years old Christian girl was murdered. A young mentally retarded Jew named Leopold Hilnzer was charged with the murder. The evidences against him were weak and circumstantial. The trial was accompanied by incitement of the press. The murder happened around Passover and the Jew was found guilty. The court sentenced him to death. The verdict was commuted to life imprisonment due to pressures put on the king. Leopold was released after 17 years in prison.

The Corfu libel in Greece: the libel occurred in 1891. Robina Sardes, a Jewish girl, was found beheaded inside a sac in the courtyard of one of the Jews in the community. The Christians identified her as Maria Desila, a Christian girl. Emotions raged among the Christians. The community Rabbi asked the bishop of Corfu to intervene, and a pogrom was prevented. About 3,000 Jews of Corfu immigrated to Trieste in Italy and to Alexandria in Egypt, and the Jewish community in Corfu was reduced by half.

The Beilis trial, in Kiev, Ukraine [19]**:** the trial took place in 1911. A Jew named Menahem Mendel Beilis was accused of murdering a boy for ritual purposes. The trial lasted for about two years. During the trial Beilis was in prison. The trial was   part of a political struggle within the Russian Empire at that time. The enlightened public opinion together with Russian scholars, sided with him. At the end of the trial he was acquitted by a jury.

The Kielce pogrom in Poland: occurred in 1946. A 9-year-old boy who was reported missing for two days told the police that Jews have kept him in the Jewish Committee House. During his stay he saw how the Jews were killing a Christian boy. The policemen concluded that it was a murder for ritual purposes to use the blood of Christian children for baking Matzot. The policemen went to the Committee House accompanied by an angry mob. In the pogrom against the Jews that ensued 42 Jews, out of about 200 Holocaust survivors who lived in the city, were killed and 80 were injured. In July 2006, in a ceremony commemorating 60 years since the pogrom, the Polish government apologized officially.

---

(19) Ukraine gained full independence in 1991, after the breakup of the Soviet Union. Until then it was part of the Russian Empire (Soviet).

That did not end the accusations against the Jews:

The sacramental bread libel: a blood libel that repeated itself over and over again in different places and on different dates.

The sacramental bread in churches symbolizes the body of Jesus. The Christian believers think that when the breads are pricked, blood drips from them.

In Paris, in 1290, a Jewish couple was falsely accused of entering the church and pricking the sacramental bread till it was dripping blood. The Court of the Inquisition sentenced them to death by fire.

In Sochaczew, Poland, three Jews were falsely accused in 1556 of pricking the sacramental bread until it started to bleed. They were sentenced to death.

The most serious sacramental bread libel was in Rottingen, Bavaria [20] in the summer of 1298. The sound of a crying baby was heard from a Jewish home. Rumors attributed the sound of crying to the whining of bread. Incited mobs gathered and started pogroms that spread to nearby districts. 146 communities   were destroyed and the number of Jews that were killed is estimated to be about 20,000.

The well-poisoning libel: [21]

Between 1347-1351 Europe suffered from the "Black Death" that killed between a quarter and half of the population of Europe. The epidemic is commonly ascribed to the plague disease. The incidence of the disease among the Jewish

Burning of Jews, 1349

population was low due to the custom to wash hands. Between 1348-1350 a libel was spread that it was the Jews` doings in the aim to exterminate the Christians by poisoning their wells. This libel sparked a wave of disastrous riots in Europe. Pogroms and mass burnings of Jews happened in France, Spain, Switzerland, Germany and the Netherlands. About 300 Jewish communities were destroyed.

---

[20] A region in Germany.

[21] "A History of the Jewish People European", by H. H. Ben Sasson, ed. Source: chronicle scanned and cropped from ISBN 0-674-39730-4 (Harvard University Press, Cambridge, 1976) p. 564-565.

The libel of "The protocols of the elderly on Zion":

This is a relatively young libel that took hold among anti-Semites in the 20th century. The libel spread to the Arab countries that adopted it in their defamation campaign against the Jewish State and the Jews in general (we will discuss this later in the book). At the beginning of the 20th century a book was published which contained protocols from meetings that were allegedly held by Jewish leaders who Head a Secret World Federation that aims to take over the world. Originally the book was written by Russian anti-Semites who based it on French writings that were not written originally about Jews. The protocols were attributed to the First Zionist Congress in Basel. [22]. The book became a bestseller and was translated into 20 languages. It was widely used in Nazi propaganda.

When the Jews realized the wide distribution of the book and its impact on the readers, they decided to disprove the libel by a public trial that was held in Bern, Switzerland in 1934. After examining the testimony of experts and the evidences of participants in the First Zionist Congress and of the President of the Zionist Organization, the court ruled that it was a forgery.

The end was apparently inevitable. The Holocaust of the Jews in Europe would have happened sooner or later. What enabled the Holocaust were the technological improvements: the railways "solved" the problem of transporting the "Jewish garbage" to the elaborate crematoriums. Now, after the European countries got rid of the "Jewish garbage", in a direct and in a hidden way, through the cooperation of the population and by silent consent, they had to fill the vacuum.

---

(22) A gathering of representatives of the Jewish nation in Basel in 1897 to discuss the possibility of establishing a home that will be a safe haven for the Jewish people in Israel.

The vacuum was filled and is being filled with full force all the time, and the day is not far away when Europe, as we know it, will vanish from the world! (23)

I have already written that the profound hatred of the Jews by wide sections of Christianity was joined by another nation: Islam.

You may think that I am exaggerating, but the answer is an absolute no! Events similar to those that occurred in Europe happened also in Arab countries.

The blood libel in the Arab world (24)

Blood libels reached the Arab countries in the 20th century, particularly on the background of the Arab-Israeli conflict. In Egypt books that contain descriptions of Jewish human sacrifice rituals were published. During the Intifada Al-Aqsa [25] (2000-2006) the Egyptian television broadcasted a program that showed Ariel Sharon [26] as someone who drinks the blood of Arab children. When Hosni Mubarak, the former President of Egypt, was asked to censure the program, he claimed that not all the Jews are the same, namely not all Jews are blood drinkers. In addition, during the Second Lebanon war [27], the Hezbollah Organization [28] broadcasted in its television channels programs that revived the blood libel.

---

[23] If you don`t understand what I am talking about, let time take its course.

[24] From Wikipedia under the entry: "Blood Libels", sub-title: "Blood libel in the Arab world".

[25] Known also as the Second Intifada. This was a Palestinian uprising against the State of Israel which started in September 2000 (from Wikipedia under the entry: "Intifada Al-Aqsa).

[26] Prime Minister of Israel 2001-2006.

[27] A war fought between the IDF and the Hezbollah in the summer of 2006 in Lebanon and in the northern part of the State of Israel.

[28] The Hezbollah is a Shiite Islamic militia. The main military activity of the Organization amounts to guerilla and terrorist operations against Israeli targets. Australia, the United States, the European Union, Israel, Bahrain and Canada define it as a terror organization. From Wikipedia under the entry: "Hezbollah".

The libel of the Palestinian organs [(29)]

A blood libel in current time. The libel occurred in August of 2009. The Swedish daily newspaper "Aftonbladet" published an article accusing the State of Israel of killing Palestinians in order to use their organs for transplantation purposes. The response of Ministry of Foreign Affairs equaled the publication of the article to a blood libel. The Swedish ambassador denounced the publication, but the Swedish Foreign Minister refused to do so. The Arab world was happy at the opportunity that fell in its lap and was quick to publish quotes from the article while presenting them as facts.

Sweden is known as a European country that leads a clear anti-Israeli line, but it was not always so. During World War II it cooperated with Denmark in rescuing Danish Jewry.

Denmark's neutrality did not last out in times of crisis. The Nazis invaded Denmark in April 1940. The invasion was accomplished unopposed and therefore the Nazis allowed to keep the Government institutions. In 1943, when unrest started in Denmark, the Nazis dissolved the Danish Government and declared martial law. The Nazis began to accomplish their plan and send Danish Jews to the concentration camps. The Danish resistance movement mobilized together with the church, the universities, and other Danish institutions, and carried out a secret operation in which about 90% (7,200 Jews) of Danish Jewry and 700 non- Jewish relatives were transported to Sweden by fishing boats. 492 Jews who were seized by the Nazis were deported to the Theresienstad concentration camp in Czechoslovakia. The Danish government kept track of them and sent them food and medications. 150 Danish Jews were killed in the Holocaust. The "Yad Vashem" Institute [30] awarded the honorific Righteous among the Nations to the Danish people "as one". [31]

---

[29] http://pediawiki.walla.co.il/scripts_new/index.php?title=%D7%A2%D7%9C%D7%99%D7%9C%D7%AA_%D7%93%D7%9D

[30] "Yad Vashem" is an institution that commemorates the Holocaust. "Yad Vashem" was founded in 1953 by the State of Israel following a special Act of Parliament initiated by Zion Dinur, establishing a Remembrance Authority – "In Remembrance of the Holocaust and of the Martyrs` Heroism – Yad Vashem 1953". Mordechai Shenhavi, who formulated the idea of "Yad Vashem", was also the first director of the institution. The site is located in Western Jerusalem not far from Mount Herzel.
The purpose of "Yad Vashem" is to commemorate and to study the Holocaust. The goals the institution set for itself: The goal set by "Yad Vashem" is to perpetuate the memory of the Holocaust and to bequeath it to the next generations, so that the atrocities and horrors of the Holocaust are never forgotten. For this purpose it deals with the commemoration and the documentation of the events in the Holocaust, with collecting objects and documents, with obtaining evidences about the Holocaust and their publication, with gathering the names of the victims of the Holocaust and their commemoration, with research and with education.
In addition, Yad Vashem was authorized by a special law, to award the honorific Righteous among the Nations to non-Jews for their courage to save Jews from the Nazis." quoted from:
http://pediawiki.walla.co.il/scripts_new/index.php?title=%D7%99%D7%93_%D7%95%D7%A9%D7%9D&dev=1.

[31] From Wikipedia under the entry: "The Jews of Denmark".

The extradition of European Jewry to the Nazis during World War II could not materialize without the cooperation of the official authorities and the citizens of those countries. I recall a reportage that was broadcasted a few years ago about anti-Semitism in Europe: an elderly resident of one of the villages in Poland blamed the Jews for the dilapidated condition of the village, even though not even one Jew was left in the village for decades.

But the libels of cutting off organs were not over. On January 12th 2010 an earthquake of magnitude 7.0 on the Richter scale hit Haiti. The earthquake hit the most populated areas in Haiti. The number of people killed was over 230,000, the number of injured persons was over 250,000 and more than 1,200,000 were left homeless. Israel was among the first countries that extended help, and the first country, also, that put up a field hospital that included operating rooms and delivery rooms. About 1,200 people were treated in the hospital by a staff of 220 persons. [32] With your permission, I will refer to this event in more detail in order to show you how truth looks and how it is distorted by a propaganda machine that uses even undisputed humanitarian acts in order to create a false and inverted reality. [33]

First to the facts:

The rescue team that was sent from Israel set up an improvised hospital that consisted of large tents that contained a lot of sophisticated medical equipment in a region of complete chaos without any buildings or any regular medical equipment. This is in contrast to the rest of the rescue teams who offered mainly first aid to the injured. The Israeli medical delegation performed complicated operations in the field, saved the lives of many and even performed births in harsh conditions.

Bill Clinton, the President of the USA, who was the UN envoy to Haiti, was grateful to the Israeli rescue and aid delegation:

"...I don't know what we would have done without the Israeli hospital at Haiti. The Israeli hospital was the only operational facility which was able to perform surgery and advanced tests." [34]

---

[32]   From Wikipedia under the entry "Earthquake in Haiti (2010)".

[33]   Since then additional rescue and aid delegations have left such as: a delegation to disaster-stricken areas in Japan after the earthquake and the tsunami that hit the eastern shores of Japan in March 2011.

(34)

http://www.israelnationalnews.com/News/News.aspx/135761#.UFISZ40a
Mo4 : Bill Clinton Praises IDF Haiti Hospital, 28/01/2010, Gil Ronen.

And now, we will go over to the propaganda machine:

There is no doubt; the "atrocious Zionist entity" has managed to outwit its longtime friend the former US president Bill Clinton. The real plan of the "aid delegation" was to steal organs from the wretched survivors of the earthquake for the purpose of transplantation in the State of Israel. The rescue operations, the setting up of the hospitals, were all a scam. The large tents, the operating rooms, all these were meant to enable the "rescue team" to chop off organs secretly, away from the camera and undisturbed.

The allegations about cutting off organs were published in an article by Stephen Landman, an American researcher, who accused Israel of committing "crimes against humanity". Landman refers to a video clip that was uploaded on YouTube by Ty West, a resident of Seattle, in which he accuses the IDF soldiers in the aid delegation to Haiti of stealing organs from their patients. In the video Ty West suggests to the victims in Haiti to be careful and to keep an eye on the activities of the military rescue delegation since the IDF has a history of stealing organs from Palestinians and from others. (35)

Jenny Ton, a former Member of the British Parliament from the Liberal Democratic Party, called upon Israel to establish a Commission of Inquiry, in order to check the allegations that the Israeli aid delegation to Haiti stole organs for transplantations from the victims of the earthquake. (36)

---

(35) THE JEWISH CHRONICLE ONLINE, Investigate IDF stealing organs in Haiti, By Simon Rocker and Martin Bright, February 11, 2010.

(36) The Guardian, A Lib Dem and a blood libel, 12/02/2010, Uri Dromi. In 2004 Jenny Ton was denounced by Members of her party when she said that if she were a Palestinian she would consider being a suicide bomber. http://news.bbc.co.uk/2/hi/uk_news/politics/3421669.stm.

And now tell me, how is it possible that "the loathsome Zionist occupation army", with its "hot headed and bloodthirsty" soldiers, volunteered to search and rescue missions thousands of miles away from its home, while the armies of the Arab countries chose not to help, not to aid not to lift a finger at the sight of the disasters that befell our small world.

Those who resolve correctly will be given the ethical code of the Syrian army written on parchment and signed by the Syrian Chief of Staff himself.

Manifestations of hatred at present

Hatred of Jews at present combines with the rooted anti-Semitism, and the Arab countries and the extreme Islam focus on its promotion. Many cartoons contain motifs of the ancient Christian hatred that have been adapted to the Muslim world.[37]

The Jew is depicted as an ugly creature, with a wicked grin, a huge long nose, evil, who has malicious intentions and whose aim is to harm the Arab nation and it parts, and particularly its children (the blood libels among the Christians have evolved around the motif of using the blood of Christian children for ritual purposes).

A cartoon published in the al-Fatihah children's newspaper of the Hamas published in London (May 2009). Its title: "The children's hunters". (From the Meir Amit Intelligence and Terrorism Center).

Generally, the use of cartoons manages to convey and express deep hatred, while creating empathy in the reader. The slandered figure is perceptible and connects to the images of evil, contemptibility and fear that already exist in his mind.

---

(37) A cartoon published in the al-Fatihah children's newspaper of the Hamas published in London (May 2009). Its title: "The children's hunters". (From the Meir Amit Intelligence and Terrorism Center the Intelligence Heritage Center (Makam).

Over time, due to a slow and visual trickle, the image of the Jew, or the Israeli, is molded in the collective consciousness and turns into an imaginary axiom of how a Jew or an Israeli looks or behaves, even though it has absolutely nothing to do with reality.

Citizens of many countries in the world found themselves, thousands of kilometers away from Israel, attacked and slaughtered because they belong to the Jewish people "and to the crimes committed by Israel". The meaning of "crimes committed by Israel" is in most cases a targeted killing of a senior figure in some murderous terrorist organization, who considers it from his point of view a right and a duty to harm and to attack the State of Israel and Israelis all over the world.

MAKES NO SENSE!

On November 26th 2008 a terrorist attack happened in Mumbai, India. One of the places that were attacked was the Chabad house, where Jewish events are held, and where Israeli and Jewish travelers from all over the world are hosted.

The Indian commando forces killed the terrorists, and then the bodies of six members of the household were revealed, among them of the Holtzberg

Rescue teams in the area of the terrorist attack in the Jewish community building in Buenos Aires (AFP PHOTO/DANIEL LUNA)

couple, whose bodies were mutilated because they were Jewish!

On March 17th 1992, the Embassy of Israel in Buenos Aires, the capital of Argentina, was destroyed by a car-bomb driven by a suicide bomber, who blew it up near the gate of the Embassy. 29 Israelis and Argentines were killed, over 220 were injured. The Hezbollah organization claimed the responsibility as a response to the assassination a month earlier of the Secretary General of the organization Abbas Musawi by the IDF on February 16th 1992. [38]

---

[38] From Wikipedia under the entry: "The terrorist attack in the Embassy of Israel in Argentina".

About two years later, on July 18th 1994, another bomb attack was carried out in Buenos Aires. The target was the Jewish Community Building in Argentina. [39] A Lebanese suicide bomber detonated an explosive device of about 400 kilograms explosive material that was planted in a car-bomb in front of the building. A large crater was rifted in the ground, and the explosion caused the collapse of the front facade of the building and many damages to nearby buildings and to property. 85 people were killed and about 300 were injured. "Injured", by the way, is an ingenuous word that conceals in its essence amputations of limbs, deafness, blindness, burns and emotional traumas that will accompany the victims for the rest of their lives.

The perpetrators of the attacks came from a well-founded infrastructure of the Muslim-Shiite community located in the borders triangle between Brazil, Argentina and Paraguay. The inquiry was conducted in cooperation with the intelligence services of Argentina, United States and

Israel. In a detailed report published in 2002, senior officials of the Hezbollah organization and of Iran were accused of organizing and of carrying out the attack with the help of local collaborators. In addition, the report finds Iran and the Hezbollah responsible for the terrorist attack on the Embassy of Israel in Argentina two years earlier.

---

(39) From Wikipedia under the entry: "The terrorist attack on the Jewish Community Building in Argentina."

The report includes among those responsible for the terrorist attack some seniors in Iran`s political elite: Ali Khamenei, the Leader of Iran and Akbar Hashemi Rafsanjani, the President of Iran, who are charged with making the decision to carry out the terrorist attack. The Iranian Minister of Intelligence, Ali Fallahijan, who directed the Hezbollah to carry out the operation in order to cover up Iran's involvement in the matter. Imad Mughniyah, one of the Heads of the Hezbollah, who served as Head of the military wing of the Hezbollah, was accused of having operational responsibility for the terrorist attack. At the time of the terrorist attack the Iranian ambassadors in Argentina, Chile and Uruguay were absent from their places of service. In the days preceding the terrorist attack many phone calls between

Iranian officials and Hezbollah officials in Argentina and between Lebanon and Iran have been recorded. After the terrorist attack, a phone call between Talal Hamia, the deputy of Imad Mughniyash, and Mughniyash was recorded in which Talal Hamia expresses his joy following the success of "our project in Argentina", and mocks the Israeli security system for having failed to prevent the terrorist attack. [40]

Another terrorist attack was the massacre of the Israeli athletes at the Munich Olympics in 1972. Members of the "Black September" squad massacred 11 athletes, coaches and judges members of the Israeli delegation to the Munich Olympics. The planner of the massacre was Abu Daoud. According to him, the operation was financed by Abu Mazen, a Holocaust denier, who has been serving since 2005 as Chairman of the Palestinian Authority.

This really MAKES NO SENSE!

"Black September" [41] is the nickname for the struggle that took place between the Jordanian army and Palestinian terror organizations in September 1970. In the end, the Jordanian army dealt a decisive blow to the terror organizations.

Many of the Palestinians preferred to surrender to the State of Israel and risk imprisonment rather than to be caught by the Jordanian army. The Palestinians know what most residents of the Arab countries know: it is preferable to be a prisoner in a Western democratic country.

While security prisoners in Israel receive reasonable and decent conditions, in their countries prisoners are subjected to abuse and to humiliating and sadistic treatment.

----

(40) From Wikipedia under the entry: "The terrorist attack on the Jewish Community Building in Argentina."

(41) From Wikipedia under the entry: "Black September".

Nevertheless, Israel is considered a negative country that has been attacked over and over by Human Rights Organizations.

MAKES NO SENSE!

The Al-Qaeda organization, that has currently an increased presence in Gaza, is glad to contribute its part in the persecutions of the Jews and in their annihilation:

- In November 2002, three suicide bombers blew themselves up in a hotel owned by an Israeli in Mombasa, in Kenya. 13 people were killed and about 80 were injured. A few minutes after an Arkia (42) airplane took off from the airport in Mombasa on its way to Israel, two missiles were fired towards it but they missed.

- In May 2003, 14 suicide bombers blew themselves up in a Jewish cemetery, close to a Jewish restaurant in Casablanca, in Morocco. The restaurant was located in the center of the Jewish community near the hotel where 30 Israelis were staying. In the series of the terrorist attacks 33 people were killed and about 100 were injured.
- In November 2003, two car-bombs exploded in Istanbul, Turkey near two synagogues crowded with Jewish worshipers. 9 Jews were killed in the terrorist attacks.

Another type of terrorism to which the Western world has been intensively exposed is aerial terror. Hijacking planes is an invention elaborated by Palestinian terrorists, who have been hijacking airplanes mainly in the 70's and the 80's.

From 1968 until 2004, 199 operations of aerial terrorism have been carried out, in which thousands of innocent people lost their lives. [43]

---

[42] An Israeli airline.

[43] From the website www.skyjack.co.il under skyjack chronology (Dr. Hillel Avihai).

In the present wave, the goal of the kidnappers is not to negotiate and release   prisoners, but to use the planes and the passengers as destructive missiles. Even after the 9/11 tragedy, there have been several attempts of attacks that failed. On December 22nd, 2001 there was an attempt by a terrorist named Richard Reed, a member of al-Qaeda, to blow up an American plane on its way from Paris to Maimi, by setting light to the sole of his shoes where explosives were hidden. The vigilance of a flight attendant together with some other passengers prevented the attack. In 2006 British citizens were arrested carrying liquid explosives. The indictment indicated that they intended to blow up simultaneously several airplanes on their way from Britain to the United States and Canada.

 We are currently among the most slandered countries in the world. Israel is presented in the global media as an occupying country, as the murderer of children, as a nation full of hate. Once every few months "peace activists", who   ignore demonstratively the massacres that occur around the State of Israel, try to enter the country and protest against the violation of the "Palestinian human rights". The media, armed with cameras, hopes to create together with the wish of the "peace activists", a provocation which will supply the flammable materials to inflame the hatred. Demonstrations against the State of Israel and against the Jews occur all the time. Innocent civilians around the globe, who lack historical knowledge, are watching constantly the animosity, the lies, and the blood libels, and are fed by them until these become for them the only truth. Israel is guilty.

I want to make you think and not to take for granted the intravenous feeding of the biased media. Hence, I ask of you to really and truly think and find instances of Jews who did acts of:

Partial list!

- Hijacking of airplanes.
- Taking hostages.
- Terrorist attacks in the midst of European capitals.
- Toppling and blowing up buildings.
- Threats to individuals.
- Issuing death sentences to critics of Judaism (the way Iran issued on Salman Rushdie, author of "The Satanic Verses").
- Firing missiles and rockets randomly on population centers.
- Jewish terrorists exploding in busses loaded with children and women.
- Jewish terrorists exploding in population center.
- Jewish terrorists exploding in crowded restaurants and bars.
- Wild incitements in synagogues calling to slaughter the Arabs.

- Demonstrations of Jews who burn flags of Palestine.
- Blowing up Western embassies because of a cartoon (on February 2006 a local Danish newspaper published cartoons of the prophet Mohammed wearing a turban that looked like a bomb. On February 4th 2006 the Danish and the Norwegian embassies in Damascus were set on fire by thousands of rioters. The following day the Danish embassy in Beirut was set on fire. On July 2nd 2008 a suicide attack was carried out near the Danish embassy in Islamabad, the capital of Pakistan. [44]

The results of your search will yield 0! Think about it!

Are the long lineups at the security checkups in airports and in government institutions, due to the fear of Jewish terrorists? Are the alerts from terrorist attacks in the world due to the fear of Jewish terrorists? How would you explain that the Jewish state that is about 0.15% of the area of the Middle East is considered as an aggressive country that threatens the Muslims and the Arabs that are living in it and around it?

MAEKS NO SENSE!

At the end of 2009 and the beginning of 2010 two serious security incidents occurred in passenger planes in the

United States. In the United States, at the beginning of Christmas, on the 26/12/2009, there was an attempt to blow up a Northwest passenger plane that was en route from Amsterdam to Detroit. A few days later, on 07/01/10 a passenger was detained a moment before takeoff of a Northwest flight from Miami to Detroit while he was shouting: "I want to kill all the Jews."

---

(44) From Wikipedia under the entry: "The Muhammad cartoons controversy."

"The enlightened world" that is used to the persecution of Jews, needs to   internalize that the rules of the game have changed, and that it is facing a cruel enemy whose goal is to accomplish a global Jihad with all the means at his disposal. By using the enormous oil money and by exploiting the naivety and ignorance of the people, he has the ability to distort reality and to turn the victim into the criminal and the criminal into the victim.

This reminds me of an event I have heard about: a British terrorist tried to blow up a plane in Heathrow airport in London using a booby-trapped vehicle. On the news he was described as "a gentlemen with a jeep". This means that the British do not understand the culture gap and the fierce hatred, and like the Western world, they too tend to judge the world from their point of view, which is anything but the grim reality. In Canada, when the mass immigration from Muslim countries started to reach them, naive policemen found themselves helpless against the waves of crime, since they were used to patrol with batons, and it took them time to realize that they needed guns as well.

You have been warned!!!

Even if we assume that all the blasphemy, the incitement and the accusations are true. The State of Israel indeed holds the "occupied territories". Well, if the size of Israel out of the total Middle East is 0.15%, then the "occupied territories" constitute 0.05%.

All the fuss is about this? Is this what they are discussing in the United Nations day and night as if more than 360 bloody conflicts do not transpire? This is what they talk about in the media as if there was nothing else.

How many times a day do you hear the word Israel? On the other hand, how many times do you hear about the slaughter in Darfur? About the massacre in Syria, Iraq, Libya, Yemen and Gods knows where else and how many, and even if you hear about them, do you have any idea at all what it is all about?

Apparently it is very convenient to blame the Jews and in the meantime slaughter various minorities in the world without being noticed, and to continue the violation of human rights by Member States of the UN Human Rights

Council. (Further details about this are included in the book I wrote: "THE UNITED NATIONS AGAINST ISRAEL").

You must have noticed that I rely sometimes on Wikipedia.

Well, is it possible that in fact this is a Jewish conspiracy to rewrite values, invent falsehoods and rewrite history for the benefit of the Zionists? Is Wikipedia an encyclopedia of malicious Jews!? All the values are the inventions of Zionist Jews?

Is it possible that nowadays, after the World Wars, with the development of the peoples, the progress and the globalization, they stop the persecutions of Jews?

No! The hatred of Jews merely because they are Jews is alive and throbbing.

Here is a small example: In 2009 the President of Venezuela imposed restrictive laws on the Jewish community. Prohibition on studies of religion, nationalization of property, etc. Why? Because they are Jews.

That same President has close contacts with his "enlightened" friends, the dictators in the Middle East, among them the President of Syria and the Iranian President.

As far as the President of Venezuela is concerned, Israel is none other than a murderous emissary in the service of Imperialism. [45] Moreover, he said that the Zionist government commits genocide. In his speech he denounced the government that harasses the heroic Palestinian people. [46]

It seems that there are not many topics for conversation during his meetings with his friends. What does he have in common with the people of the Middle East? Therefore, it is only natural that they invest their time in hating Jews.

Israel never had any interest to harm Venezuela. It seems that the President of Venezuela unloads his hatred of the United States on its Jewish protégée, the eternal scapegoat!

---

[45] Imperialism means the domination of a country over other countries and people and utilizing their resources to increase its own power and wealth.

[46] During his visit in Syria on 04/09/09 he gave a speech at a football stadium in front of 10,000 fans. From: hhtp://www.ynet/articles/0,7340,L-3772230,00.html.

The Ministry of Information and Communication of Venezuela published In November 2009 a hateful article entitled: [47] "Israel, Colombia and the aggression against Venezuela", [48] which includes references to the relations between Israel and Colombia and towards the Jewish community.

Hereinafter is a summary of the article:

Israel constitutes an existential threat to the Middle East and to the entire world (Israel is 0.15 % of the Middle East).

Israel is a terrorist country that is trying to eliminate the "Palestinian people" (the only democracy in the Middle East slandered by a dictatorial regime!)

Zionism was behind the coup attempt against Chavez on April 11th 2002.

This is a recurring motif everywhere – put the blame on the Jews!!!

MAKES NO SENSE!

Never again. A lesson that mankind took upon itself immediately after the Second World War. The United Nations was founded with great fanfare in order to ensure that the atrocities of the Holocaust will never recur. The second decade of the millennium brings slaughters in scales that have not been seen since World War II. Over 360 conflicts are happening over the planet. Memory of the Holocaust is gradually fading because of the decrease in the number of living victims. Hatred has openly raised its head.

(47) The translations in connection with the article were taken from:
http://www.cfca.org.il/article/18239 Venezuela-article-opinion-blunt-and anti-Semitic -in the website -office - information - and communication.

(48) The full article is available with the Ministry of Information of Venezuelan in the website:
http://www.rnv.gov.ve/noticias/?act=ST&f=15&t=113882, under the entry: "Israel, Colombia y lan contra Venezuela: agresi."

This book is part of a series of books I have written about the Middle East. I made sure to write the books so that they fully exhaust the subject, are informative, and free of political correctness so that they will actually present facts and truths concerning the conflict in the Middle East with the aim to show a different angle from the one that the media and many activists show out of an agenda and worldview that ignore facts and historical truths. I hope you will find this book and other books that I have written useful and eye openers that cast a different light on the reality in the Middle East. As a writer, I would be happy to get a positive review in the book website from which this book was purchased because it would help me, with your generous help, to spread the truth to other readers who are eager to learn more about the conflict that is taking place in the Middle East.

In order to enhance the understanding of the Middle East I welcome you to deepen reading the book series I have written on this subject called: "Understanding the Middle East".

The books are available through an assigned website: www.kobisha.com

Or type "Kobi Shashoua" in the Amazon website.

You are welcome to contact me directly by e-mail: kobimnsil@gmail.com

And by phone: 972-54-8030648

Yours Truly,

Kobi Shashoua

www.ingramcontent.com/pod-product-compliance
Lightning Source LLC
Chambersburg PA
CBHW060225290526
45789CB00003B/1413